HOW TO HOU
YOUR DOG IN
7 DAYS

About Older Dogs

HOW TO HOUSEBREAK YOUR DOG IN 7 DAYS

Shirlee Kalstone

Illustrations by
Pamela Powers

Bantam Books
New York • Toronto • London • Sydney • Auckland

HOW TO HOUSEBREAK YOUR DOG IN 7 DAYS
A Bantam Book / February 1985

Library of Congress Cataloging in Publication Data
Kalstone, Shirlee.
  How to housebreak your dog in 7 days.

  Bibliography: p. 69
  1. Dogs—Training. I. Title. II. Title: Housebreak
your dog in 7 days.
SF431.K35 1985   636.7′08′87   84-45184
ISBN 0-553-34615-6 (pbk.)

Published simultaneously in the United States and Canada

Bantam Books are published by Bantam Books, a division of
Bantam Doubleday Dell Publishing Group, Inc. Its trade-
mark, consisting of the words "Bantam Books" and the
portrayal of a rooster, is Registered in U.S. Patent and Trade-
mark Office and in other countries. Marca Registrada. Ban-
tam Books, 1540 Broadway, New York, New York 10036.

PRINTED IN THE UNITED STATES

CW   25 24 23 22 21

Contents

Introduction

Owning a dog is one of life's great joys. But dog ownership is a long-term commitment, since healthy dogs can live 15 years or more. It's a lot more pleasant to share your existence with a dog who is well trained and not a nuisance. Training isn't just for the sake of others, either; no one, no matter how much that person loves his or her pet, wants to live with a disobedient animal who leaves "calling cards" all over the rugs and floors. Every dog *should* be housebroken, and there are few exceptions to the rule that every dog *can* be housebroken.

My first introduction to dogs was in early childhood. My mother was a Cocker Spaniel fancier, and I grew up surrounded by the most enchanting jet-black and taffy-colored creatures. They were my playmates. The first dog of my very own, Buzzy, shared my toys and slept in my bed. Is it any wonder that when I became old enough to choose a career, my life (pardon the pun) went to the dogs? My experiences over 30 years as a breeder and exhibitor of Poodles, Whippets, English Setters, Weimaraners, cockers, and Burmese cats, as a trainer, as a groomer, as a humane worker, and as a teacher, lecturer, and writer on the subject of dogs and cats have brought me into contact with pet people in the United States, Europe, and Japan. I've seen almost every kind of canine problem behavior.

I wrote this book to make housebreaking less aggravating for pet owners. In training my own puppies, I learned years ago that dogs can be housebroken in a short time by following a simple formula: feed them regular and nutritious meals, put them on a strict outdoor walking or indoor paper schedule, confine them at night and at specific times during the day until they can be trusted to have the run of the house, and give them plenty of praise. It sounds elementary, yet during my work at animal shelters I discovered that more dogs lose their homes because they are not housetrained than for any other reason.

Training of any kind is basically communication between owner and dog, and I'm convinced that most housebreaking failures usually are the owner's fault. Barbara Woodhouse says there are no bad dogs, only inexperienced owners—and she's right. When a healthy dog cannot be housebroken within a week, give or take a few days, it's probably due to the owner's ignorance, procrastination, or inconsistency. Either the owner hasn't the foggiest notion of how to proceed or is too lazy to follow a simple training program even for 7 days, and the undisciplined dog develops bad habits that are nearly impossible to break. The owner often gets frustrated and punishes the dog, causing physical or emotional damage. Rubbing a dog's nose in any mess he makes, yelling, beating, and other harsh reprimands do nothing to further housebreaking and, in fact, only help to suppress a dog's temperament. Modern trainers hardly ever resort to force because they know they can accomplish more with positive reinforcement—that is, praising good behavior.

The key to successful housebreaking is to begin the day your dog joins your family. It is your responsibility to teach the dog to urinate and defecate outdoors in the yard or in the street, or indoors on newspaper or at any other place of *your*—not the dog's—choosing.

Please read this book from beginning to end before undertaking any of the procedures. It sets forth a specific method of training rather than random suggestions. If you read the book carefully, follow the simple formula, use common sense to prevent accidents from happening, have patience, and praise your dog's positive behavior, you can look forward to a housebroken dog that is a joy to live with. *It's very easy. There are no gimmicks. It's a strict but not a hardhearted system.*

Your dog will willingly and eagerly do virtually anything to please you if you just show him what you want. You *can* housebreak your dog in seven days once you learn the system and understand the concept behind it. And isn't it worth spending just 7 days to derive years of pleasure from a well-mannered dog?

The training program has been successful for me and for my clients. With a little determination, it will work for you. Happy housebreaking!

The Psychology of Training: Dogs Are Pack Animals Who Respond to a Strong Leader

The 7-day housebreaking formula is based in part on your dog's inherited behavioral instincts. Dogs are social creatures who readily adapt to dominance-subordination relationships. They prefer to live in groups or "packs" rather than alone. A bond of attachment formed among the pack members keeps the group together. But the bond by itself is not enough to maintain order in the group. There is also a leader and a chain of command.

Canine pack relationships are based on a dominance hierarchy, or a descending "pecking" order. There is always one dog in each group who becomes the pack leader. The leader will dominate, establish organization, discipline the rest, and maintain group order; he will seldom be challenged by other pack members. Next in rank is the second-in-command. He is controlled only by the top dog but he, in turn, dominates all the pack members below him in rank. Every member of the pack has a position in the hierarchy, and once these positions are established, each dog knows precisely which members are above him in rank and which are beneath him, and what his role is.

In all the pack's activities in the wild, the leader firmly shows the other members that he is boss. He will take the initiative in play, and he will be the first to mate. He will eat first after a hunt, but once he has his fill, the other dogs take turns at eating in hierarchical order. The leader will defend his possessions—that is, living quarters, food, and his mate—at all costs. The chain of command will change, of course, over the years. Young adults, always on the alert for weaknesses in others, may try to defy more dominant older dogs and rise to a higher position in the hierarchy if they are victorious. Younger and stronger dogs eventually assume authority in this manner as the dominant animals grow older and less healthy or vigorous. Dogs *always* inherit these pack tendencies, whether they are wild or domesticated.

The same pack behavior patterns govern a dog's relationships with humans. Once a dog enters a new home, you can simply interchange the word "pack" with the term "family." All the members of a household are part of the family pack in the dog's eyes. It is extremely important, therefore, that your dog learn his position in the family hierarchy immediately to ensure a well-trained and dependable pet.

A dominant-subordinate relationship is imperative in all types of dog training, especially housebreaking. As soon as you get the new puppy or adult dog, you or some other member of your family must assume the role of pack leader—with the dog as subordinate—by establishing the rules and enforcing them fairly. You must maintain a firm but loving attitude, and once you have assumed the role of leader, you must *always* play it. If no family member takes the controlling position, the dog will dominate, and you will end up with a spoiled beast that will be difficult, if not impossible, to housetrain. A dog in a new home will test you and other family members until he finds his place. Unless you understand that the constant testing is a way of determining how far he can go, the animal will develop behavior problems. And the problems of an undisciplined dog only get worse as he matures.

The Secret of Successful Housebreaking

You have learned that dogs are easy animals to train because they are pack animals with strong tendencies to follow a leader. The secret of successful and rapid housebreaking is to understand that dogs also are den dwellers in their natural state. In the wild, dogs hunt for food, mate, socialize with fellow pack members, and relieve themselves *outside* their dens. But they always return to their dens, snug and sheltered nests where they feel comfortable and secure, to sleep. Den dwellers will never soil their own nests, and this is the prime reason that dogs can be housetrained so easily.

Teaching a normal healthy puppy, or even an adult dog, to eliminate in a particular spot is a lot easier than you might imagine, because dogs are naturally clean from birth. For the first 3 weeks of life, the reflexes and behavioral responses of newborn puppies are directed totally to their mother. They can't see or hear until the 14th day, but they can crawl and suckle. Mother feeds the puppies, keeps them warm in her nest, cleans them, and controls their elimination. After feeding, she stimulates excretion by licking each puppy's genitals and anus. Puppies form their first social bonds with their mother and, like human babies, they respond to her affection and attention.

Between the ages of 4 and 5 weeks, when the puppies attain their sensory and motor abilities, their mother gives them less intensive care, and they become independent enough to toddle in and out of their nest. Social bonds between or among brothers and sisters begin to develop. The puppies become curious and begin to explore and play together in a lively manner. They also start to bite and fight among themselves as each puppy tries to prevail over the others. In this manner, the puppies begin to ascertain the strengths and weaknesses of their littermates and take the first steps to determine dominance and submissiveness.

The puppies can urinate and defecate now without stimulation and, from this moment, they start going to a particular spot away from their nest to relieve themselves. Puppies first become fastidious at about 5 weeks of age and begin to urinate and defecate away from their nests. If a puppy's owner takes advantage of this natural instinct, housebreaking *can* be accomplished in days instead of weeks or months.

You must also become familiar with your dog's natural excretory instincts. Dogs, like people, usually want to urinate and sometimes to defecate when they wake up. Most dogs, though, tend to have bowel movements about 20 to 30 minutes after eating. It's not hard to determine when your dog should go out or be placed on his paper when you understand these basic rhythms.

When Is My Dog Ready to Be Housebroken?

Behaviorists have determined that the basis of dog training is a bond of attachment or respect formed between animals and human beings. They say the bond is best established when a puppy is between 6 and 8 weeks of age because the early formation of a strong social bond makes a dog more eager to please his master and more attentive during training.

Most animal behaviorists recommend separating a puppy from his mother and littermates at about 7 to 8 weeks of age and placing him in a home with *loving* people. The puppy will be more inclined to become a member of the family pack at this age; he will become more attached to his owner and be more trainable. If you obtained your puppy from a reliable breeder, the puppy's socialization should have been carefully orchestrated. He will have had social periods with his mother and brothers and sisters, and he will also have received plenty of handling and cuddling by human beings, giving you a well-adjusted animal who will adapt easily to your life-style.

A puppy's infancy is very short compared to a human baby's: three to four canine months are roughly equal to three to four human years. The average child is successfully toilet trained by 3 to 4 years of age. Correspondingly, the average puppy should be housebroken by 4 months of age.

The Very Young Puppy

You can't expect too much in the way of housebreaking before your puppy is 14 weeks old, however, because he does not have full sphincter muscle control. Puppies simply cannot hold bladder and bowel movements for long periods at this age. The interval between the urge and the act of urination or defecation is very short. Unless you immediately notice the distinctive movements a puppy makes when he's looking to relieve himself, like sniffing the floor to search for a toilet spot or going around in circles, he'll probably soil your floor. Your principal duty is to prevent accidents, because at this stage of a puppy's life virtually every action is a learning experience.

It's impossible to watch him all the time, so the solution is to confine the youngster to a nursery area completely covered with newspapers in a room such as the kitchen, where there is a washable floor. Restrict him by blocking off a small area within the room with cardboard; don't give him the run of the entire kitchen. The size of the restricted area will vary with the size of the puppy, but it should not be larger than 3 by 5 feet. Make him a comfortable bed in one corner where he can sit or lie and watch everything that's going on. Just make sure his area is covered with paper so he can't eliminate anywhere else.

Start immediately to let him know what's expected. Housebreaking and paper training are two different practices. (See page 24.) If your ultimate goal is paper training, then each time the puppy uses his paper, tell him he is the most wonderful and clever dog in the world, and by the time he's 14 weeks old, he will be almost paper-trained already. If you want him to urinate and defecate outside, then don't deliberately praise him when he uses the papers. You don't want to confuse him about where to relieve himself because he's going to go outdoors in a short time. Once he's fully immunized, start taking him outside on an informal basis until he gains more muscle control and is ready for real housebreaking.

Keep your puppy clean and change his papers frequently. Don't be too strict with him, because puppies go through a fear-imprint stage between 8 and 10 weeks of age. Harsh punishment should be avoided; any discipline should be extremely mild. Do not let anyone deliberately scare or hurt the puppy. Even a seemingly insignificant episode can destroy the bond you want to establish and frighten the puppy for months. An experience that produces trembling at this stage might affect your puppy for life.

Most people postpone gentle early training because they think puppies can't learn much. "Not true," says Dr. Michael Fox, one of the world's best-known animal behaviorists. "A young puppy is a highly responsible creature with an incredible capacity to explore its environment and learn new things every day. There is a critical period between 8 and 12 weeks of age when a puppy's inclination to explore and acquire knowledge is set. If experiences and simple training or handling are denied or limited during this early period, the puppy will have a lower IQ as an adult dog." You can read more about the fascinating subjects of canine socialization and behavior in Dr. Fox's classic *Understanding Your Dog* (see "Recommended Reading for Additional Training" at the end of this book).

What About Older Dogs?

Let's suppose you already have a dog who is an undisciplined monster or that you are adopting an older dog who has never been housetrained. This book isn't for you, right?

Wrong! No dog is too bad or too old to learn. Consider this method corrective training and begin the 7-day program at once. Housebreaking will take a bit longer because naughty dogs or untrained dogs have been doing things their own way for so long that their bad habits have become deeply rooted. The older the untrained dog, the longer it will take for his natural instincts to reappear. You'll have to work harder to bring them forth, but it can be done. And once your dog is trained, you'll have to take him out only three or four times a day, and your life will be easier.

Your Choice: Housebreaking or Paper Training

The best time to start training your dog is the day he comes into your home. The first few days in a new environment are vital for teaching good habits. You must decide what form of training best fits your life-style, housebreaking or paper training. Once the decision is made, you and every member of your family must follow the formula step by step. Housebreaking and paper training a dog are two different practices, and each has its own special requirements. Housebreaking means that a dog is trained to urinate and defecate outdoors and that he is *never* allowed to eliminate indoors. Paper training means that the dog is trained to urinate and defecate on several layers of newspapers that are placed at all times in the same location inside your house. *Paper training is not the first step toward outdoor training.* Although paper training may serve as a temporary substitute for very young puppies who cannot go out, paper training is primarily for dogs who will always relieve themselves indoors, and it should be avoided if you ultimately expect your dog to urinate and defecate outside. However, the same basic training method can be used for either housebreaking or paper training. The 7-day formula is recommended for puppies 14 to 16 weeks of age or older.

The 7-Day Formula

The 7-day formula for successful housebreaking or paper training is based on 6 principles:

1. Establishing regular eating habits.
2. Confining your dog to a "den" where he won't want to relieve himself.

3. Following a strict outdoor walking schedule or indoor papering schedule.
4. Giving plenty of praise.
5. Using the right kind of corrective training.
6. Getting rid of odors promptly.

Establishing Regular Eating Habits

Regularity and consistency are essential parts of any training program, especially with a matter as crucial as housebreaking. Establishing sensible eating habits from day 1, therefore, is the first step in the 7-day formula. Regular habits encourage a steady appetite and help to speed up housebreaking by regulating a dog's digestive processes. What goes in on schedule comes out on schedule—it's very elementary.

Most veterinarians, dog trainers, and breeders agree that dogs do best on a well-balanced commercial dog food. A well-balanced diet is one that contains the correct proportions of the essential nutrients—protein, carbohydrates, fat, vitamins, and minerals—in sufficient quantity and quality to maintain optimum health through each stage of a dog's life cycle. Today a growing array of general-purpose foods—dry, canned, and semimoist—and special-purpose foods nourish all breeds of dogs. General-purpose foods are formulated to meet the life-cycle needs of all breeds. Special-purpose foods are designed to meet the nutritional requirements of special classes of dogs, such as puppies, dogs under stress, pregnant and nursing bitches, fat dogs, old dogs, and dogs with kidney or intestinal problems. The commercial dog foods on your supermarket or pet store shelves and the prescription diets available from veterinarians are the results of years of conscientious research, and they save you the time and trouble of having to concoct nutritional meals on your own.

The more a dog eats and drinks, the more often he will relieve himself. It is important, therefore, to feed your dog the right amount of food to start with. The amount of food required by any dog is influenced by breed, size, age, temperament, environment, climate, and activity level. The quantity will vary, therefore, even among dogs of the same breed. Most dog food companies list the caloric content of a food and the recommended feeding amounts by weight on their packages. These may be used as guidelines. Start with the package recommendations and adjust your dog's intake if he seems hungry all the time or if he's getting a little paunchy. Talk to your veterinarian if you are confused. He will recommend the diet and feeding program that will meet your dog's individual needs.

The Regular Routine

Once you decide on a food, it's not necessary to keep changing menus. Dogs are content to eat the same thing day after day. They also like to eat in the same location, at the same time, and from the same clean dish every day. It may sound boring to you, but it's reassuring to them. Set up a feeding schedule that you can adhere to. Put the feeding dish down, keep distractions at a minimum, give your dog about 15 to 20 minutes to eat, then remove the uneaten portion. This will teach your dog to eat promptly and not to linger over his food. More importantly, it will expedite housetraining, since most dogs usually relieve themselves shortly after eating and drinking. With young puppies, there's a very short interval between feeding and elimination. It's important to follow mealtimes with lessons in paper training or housebreaking without delay. As a dog matures, he can hold things longer and will need to relieve himself less often. *Do not let your dog have unlimited access to food during the training period.* This will only cause constant elimination. And until good eating habits are established, do not offer treats, table scraps, or home-cooked meals. Frequent dietary changes will only encourage your dog to become a finicky eater and cause stomach upsets and diarrhea, which will slow down the training schedule. You may wish to follow this feeding schedule:

RECOMMENDED FEEDING SCHEDULE

AGE OF DOG	NUMBER OF FEEDINGS	TIME OF DAY
Weaning to 3 months	4	Morning, noon, late afternoon, and evening.*
3 to 6 months	3	Morning, afternoon, and evening.*
6 to 12 months	2	Morning and late afternoon or early evening.
1 year and over	1	Morning. Large and giant-sized breeds may require 2 meals per day. Feed second meal in late afternoon or early evening.

*Give food and water in the evening at least one hour before bedtime to give the puppy time to digest his food and to urinate and defecate before going to sleep.

Water

Water is an important element in your dog's diet. It is the primary transporter of nutrients through the body, and it is linked with digestion as well as nearly every other body process.

Water maintains a dog's normal body temperature and is essential for carrying waste material out of the body.

During the 7-day period, you should offer your dog a drink of water at specific times indicated on the schedule you choose. (Schedules begin on page 41.) Let him drink as much as he wants, but pick up his bowl after 10 minutes. Your dog's water will be limited only for the duration of the training period. Once he is housebroken, he may have an unlimited supply of fresh drinking water at all times. Like food, the amount of water required by any dog will vary according to his age, activity level, the climate and humidity, and the type of diet being fed.

Until your dog is housebroken:

- Follow a regular feeding schedule.
- Keep your dog's diet consistent.
- Set his food and water dishes down for 15 to 20 minutes, then remove them until the next scheduled meal.
- Do not offer treats or table scraps.

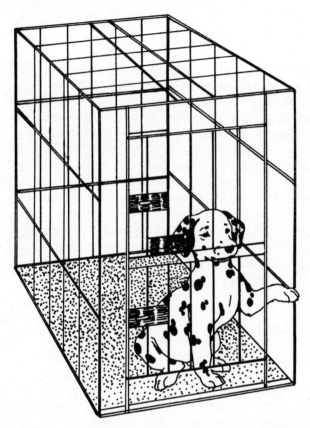

Confining Your Dog to a "Den"

The next important principle of housebreaking or paper training is based on the dog's den-dwelling instincts. You already know that dogs prefer to keep their dens clean. And since they don't like to soil their living quarters, the best way to teach your dog how to control his body functions is to create a "den" and confine him to it. As negative as that may sound, confinement really isn't cruel at all, especially when it is done properly.

Your dog must never be allowed total freedom in your home until he is completely housebroken or paper-trained. Otherwise you'll be mopping up after him 24 hours a day. Draw up a timetable, one that is humane for the dog and manageable for you, and adhere to it strictly. You may wish to consult the suggested timetables that begin on page 42. Your dog must learn to stay in his cozy den until it's time to go outside or to his papers or to have a free period. Once he understands what you want him to do, it will take only a short while until the habit is established. As housebreaking or paper training progresses and your dog is urinating and defecating where and when he should, he can enjoy progressively longer periods of freedom before being confined again. Your dog will not require confinement forever. And when he finally has the run of your house, he will have earned it with his trustworthy behavior.

A Crate as a "Den"

Before you start housebreaking or paper training, buy or build a wire crate with a door for your dog's confinement. Crating a dog is *not* cruel. It is a humane practice used and endorsed by many professional trainers, breeders, handlers, dog show exhibitors, groomers, and veterinarians. Should you hear remarks such as "I wouldn't put *my* dog in a cage like that—it's inhumane," simply remind your unenlightened friends that human babies spend a great deal of time in playpens, and nobody charges their mothers with cruelty for that.

A crate is one of the most useful items you can buy or make for your dog because it is a home within a home. It becomes the dog's den, a private place where he can be secure and one he will not want to soil. Crating is an excellent way to control your dog overnight and when you are going to be away for a few hours. You will breath easier knowing that your puppy can't soil the carpets or chew the furniture while you're sleeping or when he's home alone. It is important, however, not to misuse the crate and make it your dog's prison; animals that are crated continuously with little human contact become depressed.

In addition to housebreaking purposes, a crate is convenient for car travel. You can include your dog in family outings instead of leaving him at home alone or in a boarding kennel. A crated animal feels more secure inside a moving vehicle. He can't jump out of the car and become injured or lost; he's safe from sudden swerves or stops; he can't annoy the passengers or, more importantly, wedge himself between the brake and the driver's foot and cause an accident. My husband and I travel a great deal, and if we are driving, we usually take along our Poodle. Sparkle would be terribly unhappy without her crate in hotel and motel rooms. She adapts to strange environments easily because her crate becomes her security blanket.

Crates are made of wood, metal, or high-density poly-propylene, but the kind constructed of heavy-gauge chrome-plated wire mesh is the best choice for housebreaking. It is well ventilated and allows your dog to see everything that's happening around him. Most wire crates are collapsible and thus easy to move from room to room so your dog can be where the action is even though he's confined. Confinement does not mean isolation; it is acceptable—indeed, desirable—to place the crate in or near family rooms, such as the kitchen or the den. Puppies need human companionship, and if it is denied them, they will become lonely and frustrated.

The correct size is important: your crate should be just big enough for your puppy or grown dog to stand up in without touching the top, and comfortable enough for him to turn around and lie down in, and to stretch his legs without being cramped. It is inhumane to confine a dog to a crate that is too small; on the other hand, the cage must not be so large that your dog can relieve himself at one end and sleep at the other. He'll end up walking or sitting in urine or feces, and you'll have a messy dog and crate to clean up!

You can buy a crate at most pet stores, from concessionaires at dog shows, or from mail-order pet supplies catalogs (some names and addresses are listed at the end of this book). The cost depends on quality and size and generally ranges from $30 for a crate 15 inches wide by 20 inches long by 15 inches high, suitable for small breeds, to about $80 for one 27 inches wide by 40 inches long by 30 inches high to accommodate large breeds. Buy the best crate you can afford, one that is sturdy and well constructed. (You can also build your own crate if you are handy with tools.) Even the costliest crate is worth the money when you consider the expense of replacing a soiled carpet. One of the differences between top-quality and poor-quality metal crates is the rigidity of the bars. A rambunctious puppy should not be able to wedge his head unintentionally between the bars. See that the latch is secure enough so your dog cannot paw it open. If you have a puppy who's going to grow a lot and want to get the most for your money, buy a crate that will fit him when he becomes an adult, and temporarily block off the excess space with a plywood partition.

Most wire crates come with removable galvanized pans that are easy to clean and disinfect. It's okay to put down an old bath mat or towel if you don't want your puppy to sleep on the metal pan, as long as this does not encourage him to chew or to urinate or defecate on it. If you are paper training instead of housebreaking your dog, *never* line the crate with newspaper. A few favorite toys and chewies will keep your dog entertained while he's inside.

Try to get your puppy accustomed to his crate *before* you begin the 7-day program. Put him in it for short intervals during the day while you stay close by to reassure him that being locked up for a little while isn't the end of the world. You should be able to reach into the crate and get him at any time.

The first night your puppy spends in his crate may be troublesome. He will be lonely and may begin to whimper for attention. Comfort him with gentle words, but do not take him out. If you give in to his mournful sounds, the puppy will quickly learn that crying brings him attention and possibly freedom, and he will do it every night. Ignore him. It's distressing to look at that unhappy little face and hear those plaintive sobs, I know, but your puppy must learn to control himself. If you can harden your heart a little for only 7 days, you and your puppy will be happier in the long run. Pretty soon he'll be able to keep his den clean and not relieve himself where he sleeps. He may make a mistake on the first night and possibly on the next few nights, but he will learn control. Be considerate and take your puppy out early in the morning so he can relieve himself. If your puppy soils his crate, scold him verbally (after you take him out of it), rush him outdoors and point out his toilet area, and praise him lavishly the next time he goes there. Don't ever let your puppy sit in a crate that contains urine or feces, and never put him back inside one that is dirty.

Make your dog's confinement in his crate a pleasant experience. Never let him associate confinement with punishment. Never speak harshly to him while he's confined or discipline him then. Never crate him for extended periods. His crate must become his refuge, a secure and cozy resting place, not his prison. After your dog is housebroken or paper-trained and no longer requires confinement when you are home, leave the crate door open so that he can go inside when he wants to sleep or be alone, or when he's ill. And when your puppy goes in his crate of his own choice, he should not be pestered by children or other pets. Children must also understand that the crate is the puppy's "private room" and not something for them to play in.

Confinement Without a Crate

If you do not wish to crate your dog, you can still create a "den" by blocking off a small area in the kitchen, in the bathroom, in the hallway, or in any other room that is easy to clean. The size of the den will vary with each puppy. Some dogs can keep an area the size of an entire kitchen or a bathroom scrupulously clean, while others would sleep in one corner and relieve themselves in another. You can start by confining your dog to a small kitchen, a pantry, or a bathroom. But if he urinates or defecates there, decrease the size of the den *immediately* with cardboard partitions until he's confined to an area that meets his needs. You may end up with a den that is 24 by 36 inches or even smaller, but the *right* amount of space will keep your dog from soiling during the training program.

If you are able to use a small bathroom, kitchen, or pantry, the den can be closed off by a tension-bar gate made for dogs and small children. The most popular kind has a 32-inch-high hardwood frame with vinyl-coated wire mesh that cannot be chewed through. No installation is required, because the gate holds securely by a pressure bar. Never use a see-through gate with spaces large enough to trap your dog's head or paws. And never confine your dog in a small space behind a closed door. You'll only upset him and promote behavior problems. Make his confinement as cozy as possible so he will not bark or cry when he's left alone. (This is a particular problem in apartment houses, where whining and barking dogs can annoy neighbors.)

Housebreaking

Training your dog to urinate and defecate outdoors is easy when you establish a pattern. Dogs are creatures of habit: they like to eat, to sleep, and to relieve themselves (away from their feeding and sleeping places) on a regular schedule, so it's important to establish good habits from the start. The first step, as you already know, is to put your dog on a nutritious and regulated diet. He should eat from one to three meals a day depending on his age, consuming the same amount of food at the same times every day.

Next, since you want to teach your dog to relieve himself outside, you must establish a schedule to give him regular and reasonably spaced opportunities to urinate and defecate where and when you want him to. Most dogs naturally develop the habit of relieving themselves outdoors when they are given ample opportunities to do so. Just be sure your puppy goes outside often enough. Some typical schedules for dogs of different age ranges begin on page 42. These can help you organize a 7-day pattern that will be compatible with your life-style and result in successful housebreaking. Investing just 7 days in consistent scheduling seems a small price to pay for years of pleasure with a disciplined canine companion.

Leash Training Is a Must in Most Cases

If you don't have a fenced-in yard or if you live in a city, your puppy will have to be leash-trained before you begin the 7-day program. The best way to accomplish this is to get the puppy accustomed to wearing a collar right away. Buy a serviceable, lightweight collar. Don't spend a lot of money if your pup is just a baby; most breeds, except the tiny toys, grow out of several collars as they mature. Start with something practical and replace it as soon as it becomes too small.

Your puppy will probably turn somersaults when you first put the collar around his neck and he'll try to remove it, so stay with him. Let him wear the collar for 10- to 15-minute intervals several times each day while you keep praising him and telling him he's the cutest thing on four legs. Your goal is to get the puppy used to wearing the collar in gradual stages before you attach a lead and try to walk him.

The next step is to snap a leash onto the collar and let the puppy drag it around the room wherever *he* wants to go. Don't pick up the leash or guide the puppy the first few times; just stay nearby to extricate him from any entanglements. After a few sessions, try holding the leash loosely in your hand and follow the puppy around the room. Then try to lead the puppy where *you* want to go. Most likely he'll have nothing to do with moving forward and even pull backward and roll around the floor. Keep calm. Bend down, call your puppy's name, and say "Come" in your most tempting voice. If he does not step forward, give the leash a gentle pull. Never jerk the leash sharply, for that will only frighten him. When he toddles to you, praise him lavishly, then walk ahead with the leash in your hand. Repeat these steps until the puppy learns to walk beside you. If you can accomplish this soon after the puppy enters your home, he can be completely leash-trained before he is old enough to be housebroken.

City Dogs

Dogs on city streets should be leashed and under control at all times. Laws concerning dogs are becoming stricter and are being more rigorously enforced; it is the duty of urban dog owners to become familiar with local leash and scoop laws and to observe them.

During the 7-day training period, take your dog out only to urinate and defecate, and not for any other reason. Once he's housebroken he can go for long walks, but right now you want him to associate going to the street with the acts of urination and defecation. And train him to relieve himself as close to home as possible, so you won't have to trudge very far when it's pouring rain or snowing, or late at night.

As soon as you go outside, walk or carry your puppy to the curb so that he learns from day 1 that this is the correct toilet area. If he squats and starts to go on the sidewalk, carry him or gently pull him to the edge of the street and praise him warmly when he finishes there. He'll soon get your message. *Never* let your dog relieve himself on your neighbor's lawn, in children's playgrounds, or in recreational areas.

A female dog always squats to urinate, so she's fairly easy to curb-train. But as a male dog matures, he will begin to raise his hind leg and aim at vertical "targets." This male urination pattern is part of the ritual of territorial marking in which, among other things, the lingering scent communicates his presence to other males in the area. Be considerate, therefore, about the spots you let your male use: curbstones, fireplugs and telegraph poles can be acceptable places, but never let your dog christen young trees, automobiles (the acid in his urine will corrode paint and chrome), fences, mailboxes, and ornamental plants and shrubbery. And don't forget to scoop up feces. Excessive fecal matter is a major problem of large cities these days because so many owners refuse to clean up after their dogs defecate. It's distasteful when people have to scrape your dog's feces off their shoes, and it will make you very unpopular with your neighbors.

Starting the 7-Day Program When You Are at Home All Day

The night before you begin the training program, take your dog out and be sure he relieves himself completely. Remove his collar and put him in his crate or confine him to his "den" for the night. His blanket or bath mat and a few favorite toys will help to console him.

If you plan to crate your puppy during the night, place his cage near your bed so you can take him out first thing in the morning. *He must go out as soon as you wake up.* Don't take a shower or put on the coffee. In fact, it's a good idea to lay out some comfortable clothes before you go to bed, along with shoes you can slip into quickly, your puppy's collar and leash (if your yard is not fenced in), and your keys (if you live in an apartment). As soon as the alarm sounds, get out of bed, let your dog out of his crate, and carry him outside for the first couple of days to avoid accidents. Take him to the area you want him to use, and let him sniff around for a preferred spot. Don't rush him. Sniffing is important to some dogs to stimulate elimination. Stay close by. The moment your dog relieves himself, praise him and tell him how clever he is, then bring him back indoors. The puppy can have a little play period in the kitchen while you prepare breakfast but *never* let him run loose in the house without supervision at this time.

Give him breakfast. Pick up his dish after 15 to 20 minutes and give him a drink of water. During the training period, remember, water is being restricted by time, not by quantity, so give him all he wants to drink. Fifteen to 20 minutes later, snap the leash onto his collar, say "Let's go out," and take him to the same spot. Always return to the same toilet area, because the odors that linger from previous visits should remind your dog why he's there. Praise him enthusiastically when he does his duty, then return indoors. If nothing happens, however, bring him back inside, confine him in the crate for about 15 minutes, then take him out once more. He *must* learn to associate these first outings with the acts of urination and/or defecation, and, if he simply walks aimlessly about, come back inside and confine him for another 15 to 20 minutes before you try again. You may have to do this three or four times on the first morning, but once you learn how his "internal clock" functions, you'll get your timing straight.

When the puppy does relieve himself after breakfast, he can have another supervised free period before being confined until his next meal or outing, when you will repeat these same steps again. The length of supervised free periods depends on a puppy's age. Once yours can handle a 30-minute period with no accidents, give him more freedom by increasing his free time to 45 minutes, and so on. Your goal is to increase his free periods gradually until he needs to be confined *only* while you are away from home. He does not have to spend all his supervised free time in one room because he needs to investigate and to mingle with family members (and other pets if you have them) as much as possible. Just don't let him discover your antique oriental rug until he has completely relieved himself. If the puppy regresses, it's back to square 1: start the training program *from the beginning* once more.

A puppy will relieve himself many times during the day, especially if he is very young, and you must be prepared to take him out:

- Immediately after he wakes up in the morning.
- After every meal and drink of water.
- After he wakes up from a nap.
- After extreme excitement or long play periods.
- The last thing at night.

Between these times, stay alert for signs that your puppy is looking to relieve himself, actions such as whining, acting restless,
sniffing the floor, or going around in circles. When you see him
doing these things, try to distract him, then pick him up (if you
can) and rush him outside to his toilet area. You may be going out
8 to 10 times the first few days, but once the puppy settles into
his routine, he should not have to go out more than 4 to 6 times a
day, depending on his age.

Stick to a strict schedule. The more conscientious you are
now, the more successful the training will be. It takes patience to
make your puppy understand what you want him to do, but he
will adapt to your time schedule eventually. There will be accidents, of course; that's part of raising puppies. When your dog
makes a mistake in the house, never abuse him physically. Correct him humanely. The words "NO" and "BAAAD DOG" are
the only corrections you need. How you say these words can
convey your displeasure very effectively. This subject is covered
more fully under "Corrective Training Is Easy . . . with a Little
Patience and Love" later in this book.

Always go outside with your puppy during the training period, even if your yard is fenced in. You want to see when and
where he relieves himself, and your enthusiastic praise will encourage him. Once the puppy is completely housebroken, it will
not be necessary to accompany him outdoors. But if you live in
the city, or if you do not have an enclosed yard, you must always
go out with your dog. *Never let him roam free*.

How to Use the 7-Day Program if You Work All Day

You can housebreak or paper-train your dog within 7 days even if you work all day. Your routine will be the same, only you will adjust the dog's feeding and walking times, supervised free periods, and confinement to conform with your work hours. To

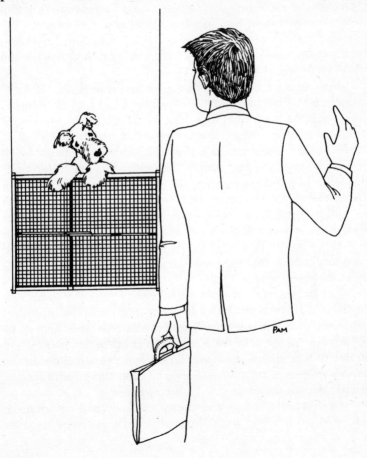

help you establish a successful pattern, consult the suggested schedules for dogs of different ages that begin on page 42.

The night before you begin the training program, take your dog out and be sure he relieves himself completely. Remove his collar and put him in his crate or confine him to his "den" for the night. His blanket or bath mat and a few favorite toys will make him more comfortable. Plan to get up a little earlier than usual for the first few days to give yourself some extra time to settle into the routine. As soon as the alarm sounds, get out of bed promptly and carry your dog outside to avoid accidents. Take him to the area you want him to use, and let him sniff around. The moment your dog relieves himself, praise him and bring him back indoors. Give the puppy a little play period in the kitchen while you prepare breakfast.

Feed him his breakfast, then pick up his dish after 15 to 20 minutes and give him a drink of water. Fifteen to 20 minutes later, snap the leash onto his collar, say "Let's go out," and take him to the same spot. Praise him enthusiastically when he relieves himself, then return indoors. If nothing happens, bring him back inside, confine him in the crate for about 15 minutes, then take him out once more. He must learn to associate these first outings with the acts of urination and/or defecation; if he just meanders about, come back inside and confine him for another 15-minute period before you try again. You may have to go out 3 or 4 times on the first morning or two to determine his natural excretory habits, but once you learn them, you can start getting up at the usual time.

Just before you leave for work, confine your dog to his den for the day. If you have chosen to paper-train (or a combination of paper training and housebreaking because you work long or irregular hours), you may leave newspapers in the den area. If you choose to housebreak, however, do not leave papers down in the den. Your goal is to train your dog to hold things until he can relieve himself outside.

Leave plenty of toys and chewies to keep him entertained, but avoid too much rawhide during the 7-day program; it makes him thirsty, and his water is being restricted. Unless the weather is extremely hot or humid and you have no air conditioning, you should not have to leave water down during the 7-day period while you are at work. If you do leave water, though, give him only a small amount or, better yet, leave a few ice cubes to melt in a dish.

When it's time to leave for work, go promptly without any emotional farewell. Don't make a dramatic exhibition out of leaving, and never show your puppy that his whimpers will postpone your departure.

You can decrease your puppy's confinement and restraint time if you can get home for lunch or arrange with a neighbor to walk him at noon. But if you must leave the puppy alone all day, come *straight* home after work. No "happy hour" with colleagues during the training period. Greet the puppy animatedly and make a big fuss over him no matter what his den looks like. It's normal to find a puddle or a mess when you first begin the training program. Just don't scold your puppy if you find them. Put on his collar as fast as you can, say "Let's go out," and *rush* outside. Once you return indoors, pick up any dirty papers or clean the den if necessary, and resume the feeding, walking, free-period, and confinement schedule until bedtime.

Keep your puppy's feeding and walking times as consistent as possible during the 7-day training period—and permanently as much as possible—to avoid throwing him off schedule. In other words, during the seven days don't feed him at 7:30 A.M. on weekdays and then sleep late on weekends, and don't confine him all day while you are at work and then take him out constantly on Saturday and Sunday afternoons.

Eventually you will return home one night to find no mistakes. And when that happens, you can celebrate.

Dogs want to be with their masters, not isolated from them, so it's important to give your puppy plenty of exercise and attention while you are at home so he does not become discontented and bored while you are gone. He should be well exercised before and after confinement. Get up earlier or allot time after work to cuddle your puppy and give him a little romp. Once he's completely housebroken, take him for long walks or a run in the park. Your dog should not object to being confined if he's toned up and contented. This time spent playing with and loving your puppy will be repaid by his faithfulness and loving companionship.

The Importance of Cleanliness and Good Grooming

One subject that most pet owners (and even some trainers) do not associate with housebreaking is cleanliness and good grooming. When a dog's paws or the hair on his rear end become soiled with urine or feces, when he goes ungroomed or unbathed for any length of time, or when his environment is not kept clean, he often becomes depressed and relieves himself in the house if he's housebroken, or away from his papers if he's paper-trained. His sense of smell may eventually become so accustomed to his excretory odors that he is unable to distinguish between his den and where he relieves himself.

Keep your dog clean, fresh smelling, and well groomed at all times. If he requires complicated clipping and trimming, you'll probably have him coiffed and manicured by a professional. But between his regular appointments, brush and comb him frequently and clean any soiled areas on his body with a dry or foam shampoo. A clean dog looks and feels good, and regular grooming sessions serve other useful purposes, such as promoting a better relationship between dog and owner, and giving the owner a chance to spot potential health problems.

I had an interesting experience with a male puppy in one of my Poodle litters a few years ago. Jonathan's mother was extremely fastidious about keeping her babies clean in the nest. And as soon as the puppies reached 5 weeks of age, I began to handle them and to brush them gently and keep them clean. Jonathan went off to his new home at 5 months of age, beautifully groomed and completely housebroken. Imagine my surprise when his owners telephoned several months later to say that Jonathan was messing all over their house. I asked to see the dog and was shocked when they brought him back. Jonathan had not been groomed since he left our home, and he was a dirty mass of tangles. After a bath and a trim, I sent him home with instructions for hair care and a housebreaking retraining program. Things seemed fine until a few months later, when the owners called again to say that unless I returned their money, they were going to place Jonathan in an animal shelter because he was impossible to housebreak. I shouldn't have to tell you that when they returned the poor dog, he was ungroomed and smelled to high heaven. The moment I established a regular grooming and bathing schedule, Jonathan never made a mistake in our house.

A Word of Advice

By the time your puppy is 14 weeks of age, he should be able to go through the night without having to relieve himself. But if a healthy puppy urinates and defecates before going to bed yet continually soils his crate at night when you start the training program, it may mean that he has not developed the muscle control he needs. Postpone the training program for a week or so. If a grown dog makes mistakes, have him examined by a veterinarian.

Paper Training

Paper training is useful:

- If you own a small dog and live in an apartment.
- If you are somewhat advanced in life or handicapped and it is not easy to walk your dog.
- For young puppies who do not have complete muscle control of their bladder and bowels.
- For young puppies who cannot go outdoors until they are completely immunized against distemper, hepatitis, leptospirosis, parvovirus, and certain respiratory diseases.
- If you work long hours and your dog is at home alone.

One of the biggest mistakes made by pet owners is to paper-train a puppy when the actual goal is to housebreak the pet. Paper training is *not* the first step toward outdoor training. It is primarily for dogs who will *always* relieve themselves indoors on paper, and it should be avoided if you ultimately expect your dog to urinate and defecate outside. There are exceptions. The first is the young puppy who has not gained complete muscle control or who cannot go outside because he is not fully immunized. In both cases, the use of newspapers is only temporary. Combining newspaper and outdoor training for more than a few weeks often creates confusion for young puppies about where to relieve themselves. If you don't switch to a rigid walking schedule as soon as your puppy is able to go outdoors, he may refuse to urinate and defecate there but wait until he comes back in the house to his newspapers to relieve himself, or to the place where his newspapers used to be. Then you'll really confuse the puppy if you reprimand him for going on newspapers when you previously praised him for the same action.

Suppose you have a puppy you intend to housebreak but one not fully immunized or who cannot go for any length of time without emptying his bladder or bowels. The best solution is *not* to formally paper-train him but to confine him to a papered "nursery" area in your kitchen until he is old enough to go outdoors. Since you can't watch him constantly, restrict him to a small area or put him in a roomy puppy pen. The confinement area should be covered with newspapers, but you're just not going to praise your puppy for using them. As soon as the puppy is totally immunized or has better control over his urination and defecation, remove the newspapers completely and take him outdoors. Many training manuals tell you that the best way to switch a young puppy from paper training to housebreaking is gradually to reduce the size of his papers as you gradually move them closer to the outside door. But I believe the best way is immediately to supplant the old training with the new.

Take the puppy out and stay with him, no matter how long it

takes, until he does what you want. If your puppy is stubborn and refuses to void or defecate outdoors, take along a piece of newspaper (preferably one that contains the scent of his excrement) to help give him the idea that this is the right place. Your neighbors may think you are bizarre, but this usually produces the hoped-for result.

The second exception is when you work long hours and *must* teach your dog to use newspapers in conjunction with going outdoors. This is a real problem because you must be resigned to the fact that your dog can use his newspapers at any time. If you envision a perfectly paper-trained and housebroken dog in this case, you are going to be disappointed. Paper training tells your dog that it is not wrong for him to relieve himself indoors, so you cannot scold him when he urinates or defecates in the house when you're at home.

How to Paper-Train

The suggested schedules for paper training are the same as those for housebreaking on page 42. The difference is that you will be placing your dog on newspapers indoors to relieve himself instead of taking him outside. If you follow these schedules carefully, you can paper-train your dog within 7 days.

Select a corner in one room—the kitchen, the bathroom, or even a hallway—that will serve as the dog's indoor toilet area. It should be a place where accidents will be easy to clean up and where your dog can relieve himself without disrupting the family's routine. Keep the toilet area away from his sleeping and feeding spots. Cover a 3-by-4-foot area of the floor with a cut-open plastic trash bag spread with 6 to 8 layers of newspaper. You are papering a larger toilet area than your dog normally needs, but this will make it easier for him to locate the paper at first. You might want to tape down the corners of the papers to keep them from sliding. It's very important to put the papers in the same location every time. Take your dog to the paper the first thing every morning, after each meal or drink of water, after each nap, after exercise or play periods, and before bedtime as outlined on the housebreaking schedules, and whenever he seems to be fidgety or looking for a place to urinate or defecate. Speak to him softly and tell him to use his paper. Every time he performs his duty, praise him enthusiastically to let him know he's done the right thing, then reward him with a little freedom. Follow the same routine every day. If you catch him voiding off the paper, pick him up immediately and carry him there. Correct him humanely and never punish him.

Change the papers regularly, but save one soiled sheet and place it on top of the fresh supply. The scent of his excrement should draw him back to the same spot. As soon as your dog learns to relieve himself on the papers, put him down a short distance away after he eats or drinks, call to him "Come," and let him walk to the newspapers. This is the time that you would be walking him outdoors if you were housebreaking him, and it's important for him to learn to walk to the paper soon after he finishes eating or drinking. Within a few days your puppy should pick out a favorite spot and start heading there automatically, and you can begin to reduce the size of the papered space. It should never be smaller than the size of a single nontabloid newspaper opened up. Make sure it's several layers thick for absorbency. Should your dog start urinating and defecating off the paper at any time, you'll have to start the training process over again.

Gradually increase your puppy's free periods as the training progresses successfully until he does not need to be confined while you are at home.

Litter Pan Training

Training a small dog to relieve himself in a cat litter pan is a practical alternative to paper training. A tray filled with shredded newspapers or absorbent kitty litter is more pleasing to the eye than a pile of soiled papers on the kitchen floor. The best type of litter pan is made of heavy plastic so it can be washed regularly with soap and hot water.

The schedules for litter pan training are the same as those for housebreaking. But instead of taking your dog outside, you will take him to the litter pan to relieve himself. Like house-breaking, you must take your dog to the tray the first thing every morning, after each meal or drink of water, after each nap, after exercise or play periods, before bedtime as outlined on the schedules, and whenever he seems to be searching for a place to urinate or defecate.

A good way to entice your dog to use the tray is to place shredded newspapers previously stained with his urine or to leave a small amount of his feces in the pan. The first few times you take him out of his crate, carry him to the tray and hold him there for a few minutes. Let him sniff the paper or litter while you say "Use your tray" in your most inviting voice. Praise him enthusiastically if he urinates or defecates. If nothing happens, put him back in his crate for another 10 to 15 minutes, then carry him to the tray again. If that doesn't produce results, crate him for another 15 minutes. Don't hold him in the tray for more than 10 minutes without success. He must learn to go to the tray whenever he feels the urge to urinate or defecate. If your dog balks at defecating in the tray at first, you can insert an infant glycerin suppository into his rectum and hold him there for a few minutes until it works. (An infant suppository will not harm your dog.) It's usually necessary to do this only a few times until the dog associates the litter pan with the process of defecation.

To control odors, remove solid wastes immediately. (If they are in clay litter, scoop them up and flush them down the toilet.) Remove any soiled paper after each use and replace it with clean paper. Scrub the tray thoroughly once a week. Even though dogs are attracted to the scent of excrement, they don't like to walk on paper or litter saturated with urine or feces or to step into a disgustingly dirty tray.

Choosing the Schedule That's Right for You

Here are some sample schedules to follow if you want to housebreak your dog in 7 days. Schedule No. 1 is for owners who are at home all day with 3- to 6-month-old puppies. Schedule No. 2 is for owners who work all day and who have 3- to 6-month-old puppies. Schedule No. 3 is for owners who are at home all day with 6- to 12-month-old puppies. Schedule No. 4 is for owners who work all day and who have 6- to 12-month-old puppies. Schedule Nos. 5 and 6 are for housebroken adult dogs.

Schedule Nos. 1 through 4 are general timetables; not everyone will be able to follow them precisely, because each dog has his own particular habits, as does his owner. For instance, some dogs urinate and defecate right after they have been fed, while others wait one-half hour or longer after eating to relieve themselves. Choose the appropriate schedule; however, use it as a model, and once you learn how long nature needs to take its course, adapt the schedule to fit your individual needs. Just be sure you are consistent. And I mean *consistent*, like clockwork.

Notice that 3- to 6-month-old puppies are given 30 minutes of free time in any given period, while those from 6 to 12 months are allowed 45 minutes of freedom. A 5-month-old puppy may be so dependable that you can give him 45 minutes of freedom, or a 9-month-old puppy may be worthy of an hour free period. As your puppy matures and the training progresses, give him longer and longer periods of freedom until he will need confinement only when you go out. The schedules apply *only* during the training program, and every member of the family should adhere to them. Consistency from the entire family will speed up the training and make your dog a better-adjusted and happier pet.

SCHEDULE NO. 1

GENERAL TIMETABLE FOR 3- TO 6-MONTH-OLD PUPPIES EATING 3 MEALS A DAY; OWNER AT HOME ALL DAY

7:00 A.M.	Wake up. Go out.
7:10–7:30 A.M.	Free period in kitchen.
7:30 A.M.	Food and water.

8:00 A.M.	Go out.
8:15 A.M.	Free period in kitchen.
8:45 A.M.	Confine.
12:00 noon	Food and water.
12:30 P.M.	Go out.
12:45 P.M.	Free period in kitchen.
1:15 P.M.	Confine.
5:00 P.M.	Food and water.
5:30 P.M.	Go out.
6:15 P.M.	Confine.
8:00 P.M.	Water.
8:15 P.M.	Go out.
8:30 P.M.	Free period in kitchen.
9:00 P.M.	Confine.
11:00 P.M.	Go out. Confine overnight.

SCHEDULE NO. 2

GENERAL TIMETABLE FOR 3- TO 6-MONTH-OLD PUPPIES EATING 3 MEALS A DAY; OWNER WORKING DURING DAY

7:00 A.M.	Wake up. Go out.
7:10–7:30 A.M.	Free period in kitchen.
7:30 A.M.	Food and water.
8:00 A.M.	Go out. Confine when owner leaves for day. Leave safe toys and chewies to keep dog entertained.
6:00 P.M.	Go out.
6:15–6:30 P.M.	Free period in kitchen.
6:30 P.M.	Food and water.
7:00 P.M.	Go out.

7:15 P.M.	Confine.
9:00 P.M.	Food and water.
9:30 P.M.	Go out.
9:40 P.M.	Free period in kitchen.
10:10 P.M.	Confine.
11:00 P.M.	Go out. Confine overnight.

SCHEDULE NO. 3

GENERAL TIMETABLE FOR 6- TO 12-MONTH-OLD PUPPIES EATING 2 MEALS A DAY; OWNER AT HOME ALL DAY

7:00 A.M.	Wake up. Go out.
7:15–8:00 A.M.	Free period in kitchen.
8:00 A.M.	Food and water.
8:30 A.M.	Go out.
8:45 A.M.	Free period in kitchen.
9:30 A.M.	Confine.
12:30 P.M.	Water.
12:45 P.M.	Go out.
1:00 P.M.	Free period in kitchen.
1:45 P.M.	Confine.
6:00 P.M.	Food and water.
6:30 P.M.	Go out.
6:45 P.M.	Free period in kitchen.
7:30 P.M.	Confine.
11:00 P.M.	Go out. Confine overnight.

SCHEDULE NO. 4

GENERAL TIMETABLE FOR 6- TO 12-MONTH-OLD PUPPIES EATING 2 MEALS A DAY; OWNER WORKING DURING DAY

7:00 A.M.	Wake up. Go out.
7:10–7:30 A.M.	Free period in kitchen.
7:30 A.M.	Food and water.
8:00 A.M.	Go out. Confine when owner leaves for day. Leave safe toys and chewies to keep dog entertained.
6:00 P.M.	Go out.
6:15–7:00 P.M.	Free period in kitchen.
7:00 P.M.	Food and water.
7:30 P.M.	Go out.
7:45–8:30 P.M.	Free period in kitchen.
8:30 P.M.	Confine.
11:00 P.M.	Go out. Confine overnight.

SCHEDULE NO. 5

GENERAL TIMETABLE FOR HOUSEBROKEN ADULT DOGS EATING 1 MEAL A DAY; OWNER AT HOME ALL DAY

7:00 A.M.	Wake up. Go out.
8:00 A.M.	Food. Unlimited supply of water during day.
12:30 P.M.	Go out.
5:30 P.M.	Food (if dog continues to eat 2 meals a day).
6:00 P.M.	Go out.
11:00 P.M.	Go out. Bedtime. Remove water during night.

SCHEDULE NO. 6

GENERAL TIMETABLE FOR HOUSEBROKEN ADULT DOGS EATING 1 MEAL A DAY; OWNER WORKING DURING DAY

7:00 A.M.	Wake up. Go out.
7:30 A.M.	Food. Unlimited supply of water during day.
8:00 A.M.	Go out. Confine when owner leaves for day.
6:00 P.M.	Go out.
7:00 P.M.	Food (if dog continues to eat twice a day).
7:45 P.M.	Quick walk (if dog eats twice a day).
11:00 P.M.	Go out. Bedtime. Remove water during night.

The Power of Praise

raise is the most effective way to show your dog that you are pleased with him. It is a crucial element in any type of canine training, and it should be administered in generous doses. Every time your dog does something right, especially if he's a puppy, flatter his ego with plenty of praise. Let him know that what he has done has pleased you tremendously. Make a huge fuss as you say "GOOOOD DOGGG" or "GOOOOD BOYYY" enthusiastically. You don't need to use the same word or phrase always; your tone of voice will convey your enthusiasm. And express your pleasure with your touch, too. Stroke your dog lovingly as a reward. Each time you express your approval, you will be positively reinforcing the behavior you praise. Dogs are show-offs and love being the center of attention. They want to hear how wonderful and how smart and how beautiful they are. Just watch how eager your dog is to please after a few kind words.

Some trainers recommend the use of treats as a reward, especially after a dog relieves himself outdoors or on paper indoors, but I don't think it's a good idea to use food as an incentive during the 7-day training period. Your dog must learn to control his bladder and his bowels and to relieve himself when and where you want him to, not when and where he feels like it, or when he gets a treat. Otherwise he'll be more interested in snacking than learning. Besides, it is not necessary to use food to bribe a dog who is eager to work as hard as he can for guidance and praise from his master. Give treats when the training period is over, of course, but not on a regular basis.

Once you understand the power of praise and use it consistently, combined with humane correction for mistakes, you are making progress toward sharing your life with a happy dog—one who has not been intimidated into being an obedient and trustworthy animal.

Corrective Training Is Easy . . . with a Little Patience and Love

t is normal for your dog to make a mistake or two during the 7-day training period and even afterward. The most effective time to administer discipline is to catch the dog in the act. Yell "NO!" and try to distract him by making noise. You can make a great attention-getter after dropping 6 to 8 pennies in an empty soda can and sealing the top with tape; the noise produced by shaking the can should be enough to distract any dog. Pick up your dog and carry him outside. If he's too heavy to carry, rush him outdoors to his toilet area. Your intent is to startle the dog so he will stop whatever he's doing indoors and finish relieving himself outside. Once he does, praise him lavishly. But even if your dog finishes urinating or defecating inside, give him a verbal scolding and rush him outdoors immediately. He won't be able to relieve himself again so soon, but you can point out the designated toilet area and praise him when he sniffs there. The object of these actions is to produce a response pattern such as "When I make a mistake in the house, I get disciplined. But when I go outdoors, I am praised."

Even if you don't catch your dog misbehaving indoors, you can still correct him. Many animal trainers say that if a dog is *not* caught in the act he should not be reprimanded because actions and consequences are interrelated and dogs don't understand discipline for past mistakes. This is generally true, but I don't agree that the principle applies to housebreaking, however, because dogs leave puddles and piles of feces as evidence. And when you find such evidence on your best Karastan, believe me, your dog knows exactly how it got there. In this instance, however, you must be sure your dog knows why he is being punished and that he associates the reprimand with his mistake. Never call your dog by name or command him "Come" when you intend to administer discipline. A dog should always associate his name and the command "Come" with pleasant experiences. Go fetch him instead, grab him by the collar, and march him over to the scene of the crime. Point to it and let him smell his excrement, then give him a good verbal scolding. Something such as "What is this on the carpet" or "That's repulsive, you bad dog!" will help to shame him. A good verbal scolding can be very effective, and the right vocal inflection will tell your dog exactly how displeased you are.

Discipline is not punishment. The only corrections that you will ever need are the words "NO" and "BAAAD DOG" said in a firm voice. Never rub your dog's nose in his urine or feces, and never strike him with your hand or with a rolled-up newspaper, or abuse him physically in any way. Physical punishment always does more harm than good, and in the case of housebreaking or paper training, it will only slow down the learning process. And though constant hitting or shouting may make your dog behave to avoid your anger, such negative actions will affect his personality and behavior and may make him despise you.

If your dog continues to make mistakes, take steps to reduce the chance of misconduct by changing his walking or papering schedule, taking him outside or to his papers more often, or giving him less freedom in the house.

Dogs Can Smell Odors Even When You Can't

During the training period and for a short time afterward, your dog may have an occasional accident indoors. It is your responsibility to clean the mistake immediately and to deodorize the area to remove any lingering scent. If you clean but forget about deodorizing, your dog will still be able to smell the odors (even though you can't), and he will return to the site of his error and use that same spot again and again. The sense of smell is extremely keen in dogs, many times greater than in man, and dogs are strongly attracted to the scent of excrement. In the house or outdoors, they prefer to urinate and defecate in the exact place where they or other dogs have gone before. It's their way of marking territory, and it is especially common in male dogs.

Vinyl, tile, linoleum, and floors with similar surfaces are easy to clean. Simply soak up the puddle with paper towels or pick up the feces, then mop the floor with a sudsy cleaner, rinse, and let dry. Several drops of a commercial odor neutralizer, such as Nilodor (sold in pet stores or pharmacies), will help remove any lingering smells. Such products are not perfumed cover-ups; used according to directions they instantly destroy the odor so the dog no longer can smell it.

The best way to handle urine accidents on a carpet is to cover the spot with paper towels and stand on them to absorb as much of the wetness as possible. Pour a little cold water on the area and repeat the procedure with dry towels until all the moisture is absorbed. Nilotex (a rug cleaner and deodorizer for pet stains) or a solution of equal parts of white vinegar and water will neutralize the remainder. Test a small (and concealed) area on your carpet beforehand if you use white vinegar and water to be sure the solution won't leave a mark. Club soda is often recommended to remove pet stains from rugs. Even though it does help to neutralize urine, I don't use club soda for this because it does not deodorize. Remove feces stains with Nilotex, a carpet cleaner and deodorizer designed to discourage pets from repeating their mistakes. If you don't have Nilotex, use any carpet cleaner, then dust or spray the area with a carpet deodorizer such as Ring 5 Odor Rid after the spot is dry to counteract any lingering odors.

As soon as your dog is trained to relieve himself outdoors, it is also your responsibility to clean up after him. Clean surroundings are essential for your dog's health. If the dog uses your backyard, train him to go to an area that can be easily hosed down. Remove his feces promptly and dispose of them, especially if he makes a mistake on the sidewalk or on someone else's lawn. Many cities have scoop laws under which pet owners can be fined for not picking up after their dogs. Piles of animal feces are not only obnoxious-looking and -smelling, but also can produce disease. They (and the soil under them) can be infested with many types of canine worm larvae that, depending on the type, can stay alive for a short time in any outside environment. If waste is not removed regularly, healthy dogs can be infected by eating feces or soil contaminated with worm larvae from other dogs. They can even sniff feces, get eggs on their noses, lick them off, swallow them, and become infected. The dreaded parvovirus is transmitted through dog feces.

A responsible pet owner is always considerate and picks up after his dog. You can buy various "pooper scoopers" from your pet supplies dealer. But if you can't picture yourself carrying such an uncouth-looking device, simply tuck a few small opaque bags in your pocket each time you take the dog out for a walk. When the dog defecates, pull out a bag, slip it over your hand, and scoop up the feces. Pull off the bag by the open end and deposit it in the nearest trash receptacle.

Housebreaking and Paper-Training Problems

There are many reasons why dogs refuse to become house-broken or paper-trained and why they experience relapses in training. Whatever the problem, *correct it immediately and positively.* Ignoring stubbornness or regression is asking for trouble. You must act quickly to prevent any mistake from developing into a fixed pattern.

Health Problems

The 7-day formula is based on your dog being in excellent health. Illness will delay or upset the training program. Kidney or bladder infections may make retention of urine difficult and painful. Intestinal disorders can cause loose or bloody stools. Be understanding; your dog cannot control runny bowel movements any better than you can. If the training program is not working, or if you notice such symptoms as vomiting, changes in appetite or water intake, genital discharge, constipation, straining, frequent or bloody urination and defecation, or fever (over 102.5° F or 39° C), have your dog examined by a veterinarian as soon as possible.

Nutritional Problems

Housebreaking problems can also be caused by poor nutrition or sudden changes in diet. When a change of diet is necessary, do it gradually to prevent upsets or regression. Start by mixing small quantities of the new food with your dog's regular diet. Over a week, add increasingly larger amounts of new food until the dog is eating the new diet exclusively. Don't hesitate to consult with your veterinarian about nutrition, especially if your dog suffers from kidney problems. Special prescription diets carefully balanced for dogs with impaired kidney function are available through veterinarians.

Emotional Problems

Housebreaking and paper-training problems can be emotional in origin, too. The arrival of another pet, a new baby, and even a visitor can make a dog feel that his territory is being violated, and he may start relieving himself all over the house.

There are several things to consider if you are planning to own more than one dog, or a cat and a dog (surprisingly, they can become closer companions than two dogs). Much depends on the temperament of the pet you choose and the emotional reactions of your present pet, but dog-and-dog and dog-and-cat can learn to coexist peacefully. With dogs, the adjustment should present fewer difficulties if the second is a member of the opposite sex. Although you may encounter a few petty quarrels, there is always less hostility between dogs of different sexes. If the two are not intended for breeding purposes, however, have them neutered as

soon as they mature to avoid unwanted pregnancies. If you must have two dogs of the same sex, life will be less aggravating if the second dog is a puppy. Adult dogs are usually more hospitable to a puppy or a kitten than they are to a full grown dog or cat. There will be much less aggression between two dogs of the same sex if they, too, are neutered.

A little common sense will get you through the adjustment period. If the new arrival gets all the attention, the first dog will probably feel threatened. Therefore, the first dog should be loved and fussed over before anything else. Once he learns he's still cherished by the family, you can start paying attention to the newcomer without hurting the first dog's feelings. Each animal needs a den of his own, and each should have separate feeding dishes placed far enough apart to avoid fights over food. Keep both animals separated when they are unsupervised until you're sure they get along. It should take only a short time until both pets settle into a regular routine.

A new baby can cause severe emotional trauma, especially to a dog who has considered himself the family's "only child." If your dog is not used to children, ask some friends with youngsters to come to your house. Observing the interactions between the dog and the children can give you an inkling of how he might behave in the future. It's also a good idea to begin an obedience training program before the baby is due if your dog is not easy to control. The mother-to-be should take part in the training if she can, because she will be alone much of the time with the dog and the baby. And when she is feeding, holding, or carrying the baby, being able to make the dog sit, stay, or lie down could be crucial. Obedience training will be helpful, too, when the baby begins to crawl and to throw his or her toys on the floor.

Expect your dog to be very inquisitive when you bring the baby home. Introduce the two gradually, but don't ever leave the dog alone with the baby. Lead the dog to the crib or bassinet and let him look while you praise him lavishly and stroke him. Don't be disturbed if he regresses and starts acting like a puppy. Lots of well-mannered dogs have been known to "brand" a carpet or two after the appearance of a new baby.

If the dog misbehaves in any way, confine him to his den when you can't look after him. Don't suddenly ignore him, or he'll be very confused. Cooping him up while everyone rejoices over the baby will only make the dog more jealous. Just lavish as much attention and affection as you can on him. It should take only a short time for your dog to settle down.

My clients Penny and Tom Young were a perfect case in point. Their 2-year-old Cocker Spaniel, Abracadabra, had been groomed at our kennel every month since she was a puppy. I knew Penny was expecting her first child momentarily, so I did not think it unusual when my groomer mentioned that Abby had missed two appointments. After the third month passed, however, I decided to call to check on things.

"Don't ask," said Penny with a groan. "We've had tremendous problems since the baby came, and now Tom wants to find Abby a new home."

"What's wrong?" I asked.

Penny described the classic symptoms of a dog who had been the exclusive family favorite and whose life had changed suddenly and dramatically with the arrival of the new baby. Despite the fact that they still loved Abby, Penny and Tom had gushed over the baby and forgot about the dog. She became depressed and refused to eat on schedule. Urinating and defecating all over the house became her way of getting attention. And suddenly Abby, who had complete freedom of the house, was shut up in a remote area and shut out of her owners' lives.

Penny and Tom did not want to part with Abby. Fortunately they realized their mistakes, and together we set up a program to restore the dog's confidence and make her feel part of the family again. They let Abby come close to the baby frequently and praised her lavishly for doing so. They made time for all the games and activities Abby enjoyed. And when Penny took the baby out for a stroll, Abby walked proudly on leash beside the carriage. They resumed Abby's monthly grooming schedule at the kennel and fussed over her when they brushed her regularly at home. The Young family has three children today, and they and Abracadabra have learned to respect each other and live in perfect harmony.

If your dog does not learn to accept your baby eventually, however, consult a professional trainer or, if the dog seems belligerent, consider finding him a new home.

Spite and resentment also make some dogs relieve themselves indoors. They become indignant when their owners leave for long periods, and they deliberately urinate and defecate indoors after they have been housebroken. Confining a dog to a small den, his crate, or behind a tension-bar gate while you are out is the only solution. Dogs, like children, can develop behavioral and emotional problems as a result of family tensions and clashes. Each time you raise your voice to another family member or to a friend, your dog can become so upset that he will urinate and defecate indoors to relieve *his* tensions.

Country Dog/City Dog

A new home can produce housebreaking lapses. Moving from the city to suburbia or to the country means that your dog probably will urinate and defecate on grass rather than on paved road. That's not as difficult a change as transplanting a country dog to a city, but in either case, you must establish a precise walking schedule and take your dog out *on time* and praise him lavishly when he relieves himself.

Dog ownership in the city is a great responsibility. You may think urban life is stimulating, but it can be traumatic for a dog with constant noise, excessive traffic, horns blowing, crowds of people, elevators, and concrete pavements. Dogs who live in apartment houses have to learn to control the call of nature not only in their lodgings but also in the halls, elevators, and the lobby besides. If you can carry your dog outside for the first few days, it will help to reinforce the fact that he has to hold things until he reaches the curb.

Often, retraining a country dog to use the city streets takes weeks of untiring patience. The toughest housebreaking problem my husband and I ever faced was when we moved from the suburbs to Manhattan. All our dogs adjusted quickly to city life except a 5-year-old whippet. Although she was leash-trained as a baby, Plum never needed to be led outside and always did her duty running free in our backyard, a quiet and enclosed acre of ground. Suddenly her freedom and tranquillity were gone, and she was forced to urinate not only on leash, but also on concrete, and in the midst of noisy New York. Hounds are known to be single-minded and, true to her heritage, Plum resisted the change for weeks. She was so unyielding that we thought she would burst from retention. She even regressed and decided that our living-room shag rug was a far better toilet area than the turbulent street. It took *weeks* of consistent scheduling, patience, and many long walks to achieve success. And when she did her duty outside, we really smothered her with praise. We took her everywhere—to stores and sidewalk restaurants—to condition her to the noise and crowds of people, too. The key phrase is *don't give up!* Plum eventually became the most cosmopolitan of dogs: she fancied riding in taxicabs and loved being the center of attention at Bloomingdale's.

Habitual Spot-Staining

Friends of mine had a Maltese named Brutus who took great pleasure in letting loose on a particular spot on the living-room carpet. They blotted, and they cleaned, and they disinfected, but to no avail. Brutus kept returning to the same spot to deposit his puddles and plop-plops. Things looked bad for Brutus until his owners decided to try the spot-feeding program as a last resort. It solved the problem, and Brutus and his owners are living together happily ever after.

If your dog, like Brutus, repeatedly urinates or defecates in a certain area of your house, remember the den dweller's reluctance to eliminate where he eats, and the solution to the problem becomes simple: *feed your dog at that very spot.* Leave the food dish down between meals to discourage the dog from returning to resoil the area. Continue the spot-feeding program for at least 7 days, then resume feeding at the dog's regular place. Should the dog have a relapse, begin the spot-feeding program until the problem is solved. Don't give up. It sometimes takes as long as 6 weeks to break older dogs of this habit. (The spot-feeding program can be used to solve urine and spraying problems of cats, too.) If you own more than one dog and have trouble determining which one is defecating in the house or off his paper, drop a little green or red food coloring in one dog's food. The color will show up in the dog's stool, and the culprit will be quickly identified.

"Dribbling" or Submissive Behavior

Some puppies or older dogs may pass a little urine when you bend down to pet them, when you discipline them, when you arrive home after an absence, or when friends come to visit. The pet may dribble urine while he is standing, or he may roll over on his back and urinate while exposing his genitals to you.

Such behavior is not related to housebreaking problems but rather to oversubmissiveness. Dribbling is a factor of submissive behavior, and subordinate dogs often do this to dominant dogs and to people. The dog does not know he is urinating; the act is an involuntary reflex. Scolding, spanking, rubbing his nose in urine, and other dominant forms of punishment, therefore, will not solve the problem. The solution is to raise your dog's confidence level and to avoid actions that trigger submissive urination:

· Do not bend over to pet or to greet your dog if it causes him to urinate. Crouch down instead, making your body appear less aggressive.
· Avoid placing your hand on the dog's head. Instead, with your palm upward, pet from under the dog's chin or on the throat. It's much less threatening than putting a hand on his head.
· Use the phrase "Good dog!" while you are petting, and also when you put down your dog's feeding dish. Each time your dog does something right, praise him lavishly and say "Good dog!"
· When you return home after an absence, don't greet your dog immediately and *don't make eye contact with him.* Eye contact, which is associated with dominant behavior, can intimidate a submissive dog and make him urinate. Look above your dog's head at first. Don't fuss over the dog for at least 5 minutes, even if he's wildly jumping up and down. When you finally do approach the dog, crouch down instead of bending over.
· Arriving guests should be warned not to greet your dog but to sit down immediately and ignore him. If the dog approaches them, they may talk to him softly but without

making eye contact. Under no circumstances should they approach the dog.
- Avoid all forms of punishment and harsh tones of voice, particularly if these have caused urination in the past.
- Obedience training will help build your dog's confidence and give him a greater sense of security. Experienced instructors throughout the United States offer private lessons (where dog and owner train at the trainer's school or in the owner's home) and group classes. You can find them in the yellow pages under "Pet and Dog Training." Local kennel clubs, obedience training clubs, humane and civic organizations, and 4-H clubs also sponsor group classes, which are usually held in some public facility. Owner and dog attend class for an hour each week, then reinforce the training by practicing at home every day.

Follow these suggestions faithfully and you should notice a change within a few days. The problem should be corrected within 4 to 6 weeks.

The Persistent Leg Lifter

The most serious housebreaking problem involves the male dog who lifts his leg to urinate all over your furniture. And frequently it happens right after he has relieved himself outside. More than likely, this beast is an adult dog who has been making your life miserable for years. Chronic leg lifters are establishing their territories. They may be jealous of a new baby, a new pet, or a visitor in the house and want to prove their supremacy. Or they may simply be showing off their dominance.

Dogs mark a territory, an object, and, occasionally, another animal or a person by lifting their legs and urinating. Leg-lifting is more common in males but sometimes occurs in females. Territory marking is a normal part of dog behavior. It is a "calling card," announcing the dog's presence to other dogs in the area and, in turn, informing your dog which strange animals are in the vicinity and how recently they passed by. In the wild, the size of a dog's territory generally indicates his degree of dominance. A dominant dog will mark as large a territory as possible, while a more submissive animal may urinate in one small area if that is all the space he can confidently defend.

Persistent leg-lifting can be corrected in some cases by giving the dog confined in a house the opportunity to exercise and mark his territory outdoors. Generally, though, this problem takes months to cure, and you must try hard to assert *your* dominance. Before you begin, you must buy a crate in which to confine your dog, and you must remove all traces of urine odor from furniture, carpets, and drapes. Try the cleaning and deodorizing hints found on page 51 first; however, the accumulated odors from months or years of previous marking will probably require the services of a professional home furnishings cleaner.

Follow the housebreaking schedule Nos. 1 or 2 (for 3- to 6-month-old puppies) to correct the persistent leg lifter. Confine your dog to his crate (or in a *small* bathroom behind a tension-bar gate) while you are at home, and take him out *faithfully* at the times indicated on the schedule. If you know your dog will not mark while you are in the house, you can let him out of his crate or bathroom den, but keep him under close surveillance at all times. Always confine the dog when you go out. If he does slip up even under your watchful eye, jerk his collar quickly and firmly as you point out the error, or pick him up and shake him if he's small and tell him harshly just how disappointed you are. (No physical abuse, please.) Then confine the dog in his crate and ignore him until the next walking time. Clean and deodorize the spot thoroughly so the dog won't be tempted to return there. This is a good time to begin obedience training; it will help to establish a good rapport between you and the dog and make you a more consistent pack leader. You will be able to control your dog's actions by teaching him such basic commands as "Come," "Heel," "Sit," "Stay," and "Down."

Don't be too hasty about giving your dog the run of the house before he is retrained completely, or he'll revert to his old habits. If the retraining process goes smoothly for a few weeks, give your dog occasional free periods indoors, but watch him carefully. Firmness is essential. If he makes even one mistake, it's back to the crate and walking schedule until a few weeks of perfect performances have been achieved. With a little perseverance and patience on your part, the dog should learn not to urinate indoors and earn his freedom. If these suggestions fail, however, consult a professional trainer or talk to your veterinarian about hormone therapy or neutering. Hormone therapy helps to reduce territorial marking in uncastrated males. Neutering, or castration, is said to reduce marking gradually in 60 to 70 percent of male dogs. Castration also makes a male dog less likely to want to roam, less aggressive, and a more even-tempered pet.

If you have experienced one or more of these problems, remember that a little patience and understanding can work wonders. Dogs are not dumb; they are highly intelligent animals who respond enthusiastically to corrective training.

In Conclusion . . .

If you have read this book from beginning to end before undertaking any of the procedures, you should understand the concept of the training program. "But it's too hardhearted," you say. "I couldn't put my puppy in a crate."

Nonsense! I've trained hundreds of dogs using this method, and they are all happy, well adjusted, and *housebroken*. Try the program for just 7 days and you will see, once everything falls into place, that it makes sense and it works. And once your trained dog becomes an adult, he'll need to relieve himself less frequently and his outdoor or papering schedule will seldom vary.

Here are some basic rules to remember:

1. Dogs are easy to train because they are pack animals with strong instincts to follow a leader. Learn to understand your dog's inherited behavioral instincts and work with—not against—them.
2. Don't expect to completely housebreak or paper-train a puppy under 14 weeks of age, because he does not have full muscle control. Very young puppies can't hold bladder and bowel movements for long periods.
3. Decide what form of training—housebreaking or paper training—fits your life-style. Once the decision is made, consistency from your entire family will expedite the training program and make your dog a better-adjusted pet.

4. Feed your dog a nutritious diet on a consistent schedule and he will eliminate on a consistent schedule.

5. Do not feed doggie treats or table scraps between meals during the training period.

6. Until your dog is housebroken or paper-trained, the best way to teach him control of his body functions is to create a "den" and confine him to it until it's time to go outside or to have a free period. Supervise your puppy at all times when he is out of his den.

7. Select one corner of a room (for paper training) or a location outdoors (for housebreaking) as his toilet area. Use this location consistently.

8. Take your dog to his toilet area first thing every morning, after every meal or drink of water, after naps, after play periods or excitement, and before bedtime.

9. In between, stay alert for signs such as whining, acting restless, sniffing the floor, or going around in circles. As soon as you see him doing these things, rush him to his toilet area.

10. Praise your dog lavishly every time he relieves himself.
11. Use praise, not food, as a reward.
12. Clean up promptly after your dog.
13. Never physically punish your dog for his mistakes. The words "NO" or "BAD DOG" are the only corrections you need.
14. Always keep your dog clean and well groomed.
15. Follow a strict timetable. The more vigilant you are in the beginning, the more successful the training program will be. If your dog is not completely housebroken or paper-trained at the end of the 7-day period, the major part of your work still will have been completed. Stick to the schedule a little longer. You'll be rewarded with a happy, obedient, and trustworthy animal.

Where to Buy a Crate by Mail

I f your local pet store does not stock dog crates, you can order one by mail. All the following firms will send you an illustrated catalog on request. All accept major credit cards.

Cherrybrook Distributors
Route 57, Box 15
Broadway, NJ 08808

Doctors Foster & Smith
2253 Air Park Road
P.O. Box 100
Rhinelander, WI 54501-0100

Dog's Outfitter
P.O. Box 2010
1 Maplewood Drive
Hazleton, PA 18201

J-B Wholesale Pet Supplies
289 Wagaraw Road
Hawthorne, NJ 07506

New England Serum
U.S. Route 1
239 Newburyport Turnpike
Topsfield, MA 01983

Omaha Vaccine
P.O. Box 7228
3030 "L" Street
Omaha, NE 68107-0228

R. C. Steele
1989 Transit Way
Box 910
Brockport, NY 14420-0910

Recommended Reading for Additional Training

Behan, Kevin. *Natural Dog Training—The Canine Arts Kennel Program: Teach Your Dog by Using His Natural Instincts.* New York: William Morrow, 1992.

Benjamin, Carol. *Dog Problems.* New York: Howell Book House/Macmillan Publishing Co., 1989.

Dibra, Bashkim. *Dog Training by Bash.* New York: Dutton, 1991.

Evans, Job Michael. *People, Pooches and Problems.* New York: Howell Book House/Macmillan Publishing Co., 1991.

Fox, Michael J. *Raising the Perfect Canine Companion.* New York: Howell Book House/Macmillan Publishing Co., 1990.

———. *Understanding Your Dog.* New York: St. Martin's Press, 1992.

Johnson, N. C. *Everyday Dog: Training Your Dog to Be the Companion You Want.* New York: Howell Book House/Macmillan Publishing Co., 1990.

Monks of New Skete. *The Art of Raising a Puppy.* Boston: Little, Brown & Co., 1991.

Siegal, Mordecai, and Matthew Margolis. *When Good Dogs Do Bad Things.* Boston: Little, Brown & Co., 1986.

———. *Good Dog, Bad Dog.* New York: Henry Holt & Co., 1991.

ABOUT THE AUTHOR

Shirlee Kalstone is an internationally recognized expert on pet care. She is the author of FIRST AID FOR DOGS (Arco and Bantam), two books on dog grooming, and numerous articles on animal health care. A trainer, groomer, and humane society worker, Ms. Kalstone has also bred and shown Poodles, Whippets, English Setters, Weimeraners, Cockers, and Burmese cats.